Early Battles of the American Revolution

Linda R. Wade

ABDO
& Daughters

Visit us at
www.abdopub.com

Published by ABDO Publishing Company, 4940 Viking Drive, Edina, MN 55435.
Copyright ©2001 by Abdo Consulting Group, Inc. International copyrights
reserved in all countries. No part of this book may be reproduced in any form
without written permission from the publisher.

Printed in the United States.

Contributing Editor: John Hamilton
Graphic Design, Illustrations: John Hamilton
Cover photo: Corbis
Interior photos: Corbis

Sources: Collins, Robert A. *The History of America.* New York: CLB
Publishing, 1993; Carter, Alden R. *The American Revolution: Colonies in
Revolt.* New York: Franklin Watts, 1988; Dolan, Edward. *American Revolution:
How We Fought the War of Independence.* Brookfield, Connecticut: The
Millbrook Press, 1995; Gay, Kathlyn. *Revolutionary War.* New York: Twenty-
First Century Books, A Division of Henry Holt and Company, Inc., 1995;
Grant, R. G. *The American Revolution.* New York: Thomas Learning, 1995;
Heinrichs, Ann. *America the Beautiful: Rhode Island.* Chicago: Childrens
Press, 1990; Kent, Keborah. *America the Beautiful: Massachusetts.* Chicago:
Childrens Press, 1988; Kent, Deborah. *America the Beautiful: Pennsylvania.*
Chicago: Childrens Press, 1988; Lukes, Bonnie L. *World History Series: The
American Revolution.* San Diego: Lucent Books, 1996; McNair, Sylvia.
America the Beautiful: Vermont. Chicago: Childrens Press, 1991; Stewart, Gail.
The Revolutionary War. San Diego: Lucent Books, 1991; Van Zandt, Eleanor.
A History of the United States Through Art. New York: Thomson Learning,
1996.

Library of Congress Cataloging–in–Publication Data

Wade, Linda R.
    Early Battles of the American Revolution / Linda R. Wade
        p. cm. -- (The American Revolution)
    Includes bibliographical references (p.) and index.
    ISBN 1-57765-155-3
    1. United States--History--Revolution, 1775-1783--Campaigns--Juvenile
literature. [1. United States--History--Revolution, 1775-1783]. I. Title.
E230.W27 2001
973.3'3--dc21
                                                        00--56907

CONTENTS

INTRODUCTION

For 150 years the American colonies enjoyed a good relationship with the Mother Country of England. Then the English Parliament needed money. The colonies became a source of funds to pay previous war debts, as well as British soldiers. They had been stationed in North America in 1763 after the French and Indian War.

The British decided that these needed funds could come from various taxes levied on the colonists. The people were angry. When a patrolling squad of British soldiers met some of these angry colonists, there was a fight. Five Americans died. This clash was called the Boston Massacre. England repealed some of the tax acts.

In 1773, tax still remained on tea. The Sons of Liberty went into action. These patriots, dressed as Native Americans, boarded three ships and dumped tea in the Boston Harbor. England answered by closing the harbor.

Suddenly, revolt, revolution, and war was the talk in the taverns, shops, and homes of the colonies. What would happen next?

Left: The Boston Tea Party, December 16, 1773.

Facing page: British soldiers fire on a crowd of unarmed colonists at the Boston Massacre.

Chapter 1

Lexington and Concord

In almost every city a band of men formed a militia. Farmers and shopkeepers brought out their hunting guns and practiced drills. These armed civilians were called minutemen, because they swore to be ready to fight at a minute's notice. Sam Adams and John Hancock were the leaders. The minutemen from Massachusetts began collecting military supplies and storing them at Concord.

With all this activity, General Thomas Gage, the British governor, became alarmed. He decided to seize the stored supplies in Lexington, 15 miles west of Boston. This would end the threats to the British soldiers. He also wanted to capture Adams and Hancock. He thought that the capture of these radicals would quash a rebellion before it could get started.

The Americans had spies who learned about the orders to attack. They warned Adams and Hancock, who then fled from Boston to avoid being captured. Although Gage realized he could not catch up with them, he was determined to capture their ammunition.

The British could get to Concord two different ways. They could go the long way by land. They could also cross the Charles River

Facing page: A statue by Daniel Chester French at the Old North Bridge in Concord, Massachusetts commemorates the minutemen who stood their ground against the British on April 19, 1775.

Paul Revere rides on a moonlit Massachusetts road in order to warn the American forces of British troop movements.

and then march to Concord. Since the colonists were unsure of the route, Paul Revere used a code system. If the British decided to go by water, two lanterns would shine in Boston's Old North Church. If the British chose the land route, only one lantern would be lit.

On April 17, 1775, William Dawes and Dr. Samuel Prescott were sent to spread the alarm all the way to Concord. No one knew yet which route the British would take.

On April 18, the minutemen realized that the British were moving by boat. After making sure that two lanterns were hung in the church tower, Paul Revere rushed to a small boat he had placed on the Charles River. He moved through the water quickly. His friends had a fast horse ready to go when he arrived on the Charlestown shore. Quickly, Revere set off at a gallop to warn Americans.

The British troops were several miles from Paul Revere. As he spread the word, church bells rang. Alarm guns and drums sounded. Beacons flashed in the night. He continued to bang on doors and call out to the people. "The British are coming! The British are coming!"

On April 19, about 70 minutemen awaited the arrival of the British soldiers in Lexington. At dawn about 400 British troops arrived. There were far more redcoats than the minutemen expected. The minutemen were ordered to retreat.

As they were leaving, a shot rang out. The British answered with rifle fire and a charge with bayonets. No one knows who fired that first shot, but soon eight Americans were dead and 10 lay wounded.

The British then marched on to Concord. Here they found some wooden carts used to hold cannons. They burned the carts. The smoke made the minutemen think the British were burning the city. The minutemen were very angry. A group of them fired at the redcoats guarding the Old North Bridge. The British fought off the attack and headed back to Boston.

The minutemen gathered and hid in the woods and behind stone walls, shooting at the British from these hidden posts. The British were shocked and did not know how to fight this unseen enemy. They suffered a humiliating defeat.

Finally, the British soldiers arrived back in Boston. Seventy-two men died and nearly 200 more were wounded in the day's fighting. The Americans lost 49 lives. Few thought it possible that they had boldly attacked and defeated the British.

Neither the British soldiers nor the colonists had looked for battle, but that day it had happened. The encounter announced that the colonists meant to fight the British for their rights. Those shots started a long war that ended in American independence.

Colonists fight at the Battle of Concord.

CHAPTER 2

PREPARATIONS FOR WAR

On April 23, 1775, Massachusetts gathered 13,600 soldiers. Volunteers from the northern colonies assembled and headed for Boston. They established camps around the city and began a yearlong siege of British-held Boston.

The colonists now realized that freedom meant a separation from their home country. It was difficult for some of the people. Many had family members in England. Many liked the idea of a king. What they did not like were the new rules and regulations. They did not like the changes that England was forcing upon them.

It was mainly the leaders who saw war as the only way to achieve freedom. Preparations went forward quickly. They had to be ready to meet the redcoats at every turn.

Men dressed in 18th century American military costume fire muskets during a Revolutionary War battle reenactment.

Chapter 3

Guns From Fort Ticonderoga

Fort Ticonderoga was a little place on Lake Champlain in New York State. It was also an important British stronghold. On May 10, 1775, Ethan Allen and Benedict Arnold led a group of about 200 Vermont soldiers on a surprise attack. These soldiers were called the Green Mountain Boys.

There were no deaths in this surprise attack, but it was a great victory for the Americans. They needed the captured cannons of Fort Ticonderoga to fight the British at Boston.

The men faced a very difficult task in moving the cannons. Finally, they placed the heavy artillery on wagons so that oxen and very strong horses could take it to Boston. Both the men and animals struggled through deep snows. They climbed mountains. They ran so low on supplies that they ate their leather moccasins.

But they were successful. They arrived in Boston in time to surround the city and force the redcoats to retreat.

A cannon at Fort Ticonderoga overlooking Lake Champlain.

CHAPTER 4

SECOND CONTINENTAL CONGRESS

O n May 10, three weeks after the clash in Lexington and Concord, the Second Continental Congress met in the Pennsylvania State House. Some of the most influential patriots were present. Sam Adams, John Adams, and John Hancock came from

An actor in historical costume sits next to the silver Synge inkwell that was used to sign the Declaration of Independence and the United States Constitution in Independence Hall.

Actors in historical costumes portray America's founding fathers as they recreate the drafting of the Declaration of Independence in the Assembly Room of Independence Hall.

Massachusetts. Benjamin Franklin represented Pennsylvania. Patrick Henry and George Washington came from Virginia.

The men who attended did not seek a complete break with Britain. They were trying to find a way to make peace. They hoped to head off a full-scale war. However, to protect themselves, they created an army and navy.

Perhaps the most important result of this meeting was that the colonies saw themselves as one unit. There were still colonists who were against the whole idea of independence. However, by now, many of the colonists were calling themselves Americans.

Thomas Jefferson began the process of writing the Declaration of Independence. He said that the colonists were no longer subject to British rule. He used the term "United States of America" for the first time.

CHAPTER 5

THE BATTLE OF BUNKER HILL

During May 1775, reinforcements arrived from England. With these troops came three more generals: William Howe, John Burgoyne, and Henry Clinton. They convinced General Gage that he needed to take control of a place called Bunker Hill (actually Breed's Hill). It was located in Boston on the nearby Charlestown peninsula. They feared that the patriots would set up guns and control the area.

Rumors of war were passed around constantly. It was the topic of conversation in all the meeting places. The townspeople were fascinated by this talk of battle.

Then, on June 17, 1775, it happened. The patriot soldiers had dug trenches and were prepared in the event of an attack. People gathered on the high points of Boston to watch all the activities.

They saw the redcoats begin their march. They came in straight lines. Militiamen waited behind walls of dirt and stone. They were ordered not to fire "until you can see the whites of their eyes."

When the British were only 15 paces away, the order came. Colonists fired their guns and the battle began. Lines of British soldiers fell to the ground.

Another line of redcoats came. Line after line fell to the thunderous roar of the patriots' guns.

When the third attack came 30 minutes later, the colonists ran out of ammunition. All they had were bayonets and stones to defend themselves. The British soon broke through. Even though the colonists had driven the British back twice, they had to run for their lives. Militiamen fell bleeding and dying while trying to flee from the British. It was one of the fiercest battles of the whole war.

Over 400 Americans were killed or wounded. However, the British lost more than 1,000 men. Even though the British won the battle, their loss of soldiers was devastating, accounting for about half of their army.

American colonists and British soldiers fight at the top of Breed's Hill (Bunker Hill). The battle was a victory for the British, but they lost many more men than the colonists.

Chapter 6

General Washington Takes Charge

George Washington was a wealthy Virginia landowner. He was also a great leader. Members of the Continental Congress recognized his abilities. On June 15, Washington was asked to be commander-in-chief of the new Continental Army.

Esek Hopkins became commander-in-chief of the Continental Navy. Washington named Nathanael Greene as his second-in-command. In July, 1775, General Washington made his headquarters at Cambridge, Massachusetts. This was a little village on the western bank of the Charles River.

Washington knew that his new army would be made up of undisciplined militia. There were farmers, storekeepers, fishermen, and craftsmen. Some had fought on the frontier and in the French

George Washington takes command of the Continental Army at Cambridge, 1775.

General George Washington demonstrating how to fire a cannon.

and Indian War. The ways of war were different. They were familiar with hide-and-seek fighting.

Washington began training the 20,000 men who gathered. He had to teach them to fight the well-disciplined British army. He put them through drills. He marched them for hours. They had little time for themselves. He knew that this hard training was necessary if they were to defeat the famous British army.

In order for Washington to have the kind of army that he needed, he set some strict rules. He punished soldiers who did not follow his orders.

Often the new soldiers stayed with the army for only a short time and then walked away. For this reason, it was difficult for Washington to plan his battle strategy. He was never sure of how many men he would have.

Chapter 7

The British Army

While George Washington's army consisted of mostly first-time soldiers, the British army was made up of professional soldiers. They were well trained by experienced officers. They had new weapons. They also had help. The British used mercenaries, or hired soldiers, to fight on their side. These soldiers were Hessians, from the Hesse region of Germany. The Native Americans wanted to fight with the British. Many tribes hated the colonists because settlers had taken over their lands.

The big problem for the British army was its distance from home. Supplies were often late. The men became restless so far from home.

Men dressed as British soldiers shoot their rifles in a reenactment of the American Revolutionary War.

CHAPTER 8

DIVISION IN THE COLONIES

These were difficult times for the people living in the colonies. While their hearts were with the mother country of England, their eager spirits longed for the freedoms offered by their new home country. Many stayed loyal to the king. Others wanted a complete break.

Most of the colonists still did not want war. Even family members disagreed. They all wanted to find some way to solve the problems. The colonists who were totally opposed to the Revolution were called Tories.

Complete freedom from Britain was hard to consider. Their language, their laws, and their customs were British. Many people had relatives in Britain. Most colonial trade was with Britain or with British colonies in the West Indies. The British navy had protected the American ships.

To fight an all-out war with Britain seemed impossible. How could they ever hope to win? Many colonists were very fearful of this thing called "independence." Colonists struggled within themselves for answers to the puzzling questions.

CHAPTER 9

THE WRITINGS THAT CHANGED MINDS

Thomas Paine wrote a book early in 1776. In it he said that King George III was a bully. He called him the "Royal Brute of Britain." Paine felt that people should rule themselves. He suggested that the colonists who remained loyal to England had no "common sense."

Over 120,000 copies of Paine's book sold by June 1776. It became a best-seller. More and more colonists began to favor a complete break with England.

After reading this pamphlet, Richard Henry Lee of Virginia gave a speech to Congress on June 7, 1776. He said, "These United Colonies are and of Right ought to be Free and Independent States."

Phillis Wheatley was a black slave who wrote poetry. She had been kidnapped when she was only five or six years old and brought to this country. She compared slavery to the conditions of colonists under British rule.

A color line-cut illustration of American poet Phyllis Wheatley (1753?-1784), seated at her desk.

A statue of Thomas Paine presented to the People of England from the Thomas Paine Foundation, New York.

A song became the battle cry for the patriots. Fife players played "Yankee Doodle." Soldiers and colonists sang it. The British soldiers mocked the patriots when they marched to Lexington and Concord. Then came word that King Louis XVI of France offered one million dollars in arms and munitions to America. Spain also promised support to the colonies.

CHAPTER 10

THE DECLARATION OF INDEPENDENCE

The Congress waited almost a month before voting on a separation from England. While the uncertain colonies were still deciding what to do, a committee was selected to draw up a Declaration of Independence.

Thomas Jefferson, a lawyer from Virginia, was chosen to begin the document. He worked on it every day. He rewrote it many times. He wanted the words to be right.

The United States Declaration of Independence.

The signing of the Declaration of Independence, July 4, 1776.

In the introduction, Jefferson suggested that sometimes people must cut themselves off from the country they once belonged to. They must have good reasons for this action.

He went on to say, "We hold these truths to be self-evident, that all men are created equal, that they are endowed by their Creator with certain unalienable Rights, that among these are Life, Liberty, and the pursuit of Happiness."

Then Jefferson listed the unfair things that the king and Parliament had done.

Finally, he said that the 13 colonies were no longer a part of Great Britain. He declared, "that these United Colonies are, and of Right ought to be Free and Independent States."

On June 28, the document was read to Congress. After several small changes were made, it was approved on July 4, 1776. The 13 colonies had declared independence. A new nation had been born.

CHAPTER 11

THE BATTLE OF LONG ISLAND

Washington did not want to make a stand in the area of New York City. The islands of Manhattan and Long Island were difficult to defend. It was a large area and water separated the troops. However, Congress wanted Washington to hold the area.

Men dressed as British troops fire their weapons during a Revolutionary War reenactment.

The British sailed up the Hudson River on August 27, 1776. General Howe had 15,000 soldiers. Washington was outnumbered two to one. He suffered a severe defeat and his army retreated back to Brooklyn Heights. They faced possible capture by the British, or even total surrender.

But that night, Washington put his soldiers in small boats on the East River. They went to Manhattan Island and then New York City. Then the army went to Harlem Heights. Washington avoided large-scale battles with the British by a series of retreats. There were little skirmishes from place to place.

On September 11, a peace conference was held on Staten Island with British Admiral Lord Richard Howe. John Adams and Benjamin Franklin listened as Howe demanded that the colonists revoke the Declaration of Independence. Adams and Franklin refused, putting an end to the conference.

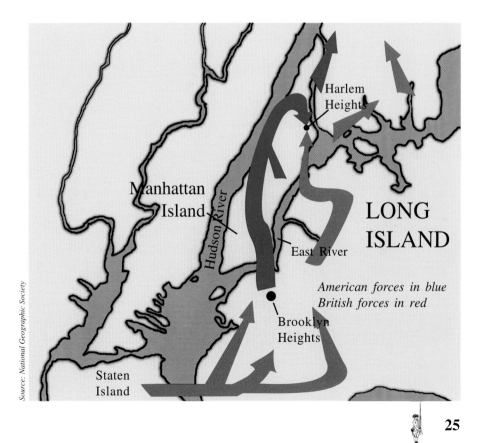

Source: National Geographic Society

Harlem Heights

Manhattan Island

Hudson River

East River

LONG ISLAND

American forces in blue British forces in red

Brooklyn Heights

Staten Island

CHAPTER 12

NATHAN HALE

Nathan Hale was a young captain in the Continental Army. He was a good leader. He helped in capturing a supply-loaded vessel from under the guns of a British warship, and then was selected to fight in a group called the Rangers. The Rangers were known for their daring leadership and fighting qualities in dangerous missions.

As a Ranger, he volunteered to pass through the British lines and get information on the British position. He was successful getting the information. However, as Hale returned on September 21, 1776, the British captured him.

Hale was taken before General William Howe, the British commander. He was condemned to hang the next day as a spy.

His final words were, "I only regret that I have but one life to lose for my country."

Nathan Hale is led to his execution by the British.

CHAPTER 13

THE BATTLE OF TRENTON

A discouraged American army was faltering. Soldiers deserted. General Washington found it difficult to get new recruits. Half the people had never really supported the rebellion, and now they infected the rest. It looked as though the new republic was on its last leg.

The situation was desperate. Even British General William Howe considered the campaign of 1776 over because the Americans had been retreating for six months. Washington knew he must do something to rally his troops. It was the only way to keep the cause alive.

George Washington stands tall as his boat crosses turbulent water in the Delaware River in 1776.

On December 22, 1776, Washington had 4,707 men fit for duty. He called his staff together. He said there was to be a surprise attack on the Hessian garrison across the river at Trenton, New Jersey. Washington began moving his troops on Christmas night, when it was least expected.

Fighting a blinding snowstorm and severe cold, the soldiers approached the river. Some of the soldiers were barefooted. They had wrapped rags around their feet.

Quietly the men boarded the freight boats and crossed the Delaware River. By 3:00 a.m. all of the men and their guns were safely across. Swiftly, they advanced in two columns on the little town of 100 houses.

It was 8:00 a.m. The men soon killed the guards and set up their guns before the Germans could awaken. The enemy tried to resist but quickly lost 40 to 60 men, causing the Hessian commanders to surrender. Washington took 900 prisoners, losing only four wounded men and two who later froze to death on the bitter return march.

On January 3, Washington made another attack. He defeated three regiments of a British force in the Battle of Princeton. He then took up a strong position on high ground at Morristown in north central New Jersey.

These victories brought hope to the colonists. It also added new soldiers to the American cause. In three weeks, Washington had reversed all that General Howe had accomplished.

Washington's crossing of the Delaware was a crucial turning point in the War of Independence. Americans now felt that they had a chance of defeating the mighty British army.

INTERNET SITES

ushistory.org
http://www.ushistory.org/

This Internet exploration of the Revolutionary War is presented by the Independence Hall Association. Visitors can learn interesting facts about many aspects of the war, including major battles, biographies of important patriots (Ben Franklin, Betsy Ross, Thomas Paine, and others), plus information on historic sites that can be toured today. The section on the Declaration of Independence includes photos of the document, as well as biographies of the signers and Jefferson's account of the writing.

Liberty! The American Revolution
http://www.pbs.org/ktca/liberty/

The official online companion to "Liberty! The American Revolution," a series of documentaries originally broadcast on PBS in 1997. Includes timelines, resource material, and related topics—a potpourri of information on the American Revolution. Topics cover daily life in the colonies, the global village, a military point of view, plus a section on the making of the TV series. Also includes a "Revolutionary Game."

These sites are subject to change. Go to your favorite search engine and type in "American Revolution" for more sites.

PASS IT ON

American Revolutionary War buffs: educate readers around the country by passing on interesting information you've learned about the American Revolution. Maybe your family visited a famous Revolutionary War battle site, or you've taken part in a reenactment. Who's your favorite historical figure from the Revolutionary War? We want to hear from you!

To get posted on the ABDO Publishing Company Web site, email us at "History@abdopub.com"

Visit the ABDO Publishing Web site at www.abdopub.com

GLOSSARY

18th Century

The years from 1700 to 1799.

Acts

Laws.

Bayonet

A sharp knife fastened to a musket and used in hand-to-hand combat.

Casualties

Soldiers who are killed or wounded.

Colonists

A group of people who leave their country to live in a land far away.

Continental Army

The American army led by George Washington.

Continental Congress

A group of lawmakers in the Colonies at the time of the American Revolution.

Colony

A territory, or land, that is far from the country that rules it.

Declaration of Independence

The official statement issued by the American colonists declaring freedom to govern themselves.

King George III

The King of England at the time of the American Revolution.

Militia

Citizens who were part-time soldiers rather than professional army fighters. Militiamen usually fought only in their local area and continued with their normal jobs when they were not needed.

Minutemen

American civilians who could be "ready to fight in a minute."

Musket

Muzzle-loading black powder rifle.

Patriots

Americans who believed they had a right to stand up for their liberties.

Rebel

Another name for Patriot.

Rebellion

An armed fight against one's own government.

Repeal

To officially do away with.

Retreat

When an army turns around and goes back instead of forward.

Sons of Liberty

Groups of colonists who organized themselves to fight the British.

Tories

Colonists who remained loyal to Great Britain.

A lithograph of the fife and drum players of A.M. Willard's famous painting.

INDEX